Everyone

written by Joelie Croser
illustrated by Kelly Gates

"Here I am," said Mother Bird. "I've got worms for everyone."

She sat on the edge of her nest and opened her beak wide. The three baby birds gobbled down all the worms.

"We're still hungry," they said.

"You're always hungry," said Mother Bird as she flew away for more worms.

Suddenly a big frog jumped into the nest.

"Who are you?" asked the baby birds.

"I'm a frog, and my name is Everyone," said the frog.

"That's a funny name," said the smallest baby bird.

The frog stared at the little bird. "I'm going to live in this nest, but you had better not tell anyone," he said.

A fly went by. The frog zapped it and gulped it down.

"That's what I'll do to anyone who tells," he said.

5

The baby birds huddled together.

"Don't worry," whispered the biggest baby bird to the others. "Mother is coming."

"Here I am," called Mother Bird. "I've got worms for everyone."

She opened her beak. The big frog glared at the baby birds and gobbled down all the worms. Then he hid under the baby birds.

"We're still hungry," said the baby birds.

"You're always hungry," said Mother Bird,
and off she flew.

Mother Bird came back three more times that morning. Each time the same thing happened, and Everyone, the greedy frog, ate all the worms.

"What are we going to do?" said the middle-sized baby bird.

"What can we do?" said the smallest one. He shivered as he remembered the fly.

"We must do something," said the biggest baby bird. She looked at her wings. They had a few long feathers now.

"I'm going out," she whispered. "I'll wait till the wind blows so you can say that the wind took me away."

Later that day, the wind came. The biggest baby bird climbed over the edge of the nest and opened her wings. The wind carried her gently down to the ground.

Mother Bird saw her there.

"What are you doing?" she cried.

The baby bird told her about the big frog. It made Mother Bird very angry.

"Climb onto my back, and I'll take you up to the nest," she said. "Tell the others to do as I say. Just trust me," she said.

Soon the baby bird was back in her nest. Mother Bird flew off for more worms so the frog would not guess that they had a plan. But as soon as Everyone had gobbled down the next batch of worms, Mother Bird said, "It's time for you all to fly."

"How?" said the baby birds.

"Just hop out of the nest and stand on the branch," said mother bird.

"What happens then?" asked a baby bird.

"First I'll check that the nest is empty," said Mother Bird. "I need ALL of you on the branch. Then I'll fly behind you and push you all off. Just open your wings and flap."

One, two, three! The baby birds hopped out of the nest and stood on the branch.

"Nobody will push **me** off a branch," said Everyone, the frog. He hopped out of the nest and down the tree as fast as he could go.

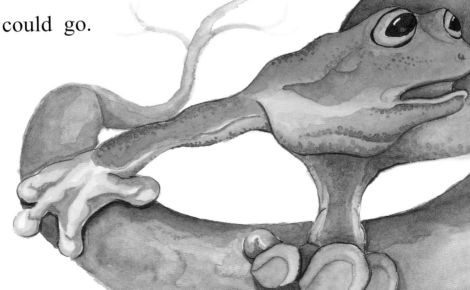

The little birds laughed and hopped back into the nest.

"Now who is hungry?" said Mother Bird.

"Everyone!" said the baby birds.